A Primer
for the Gaited Horse
and Rider

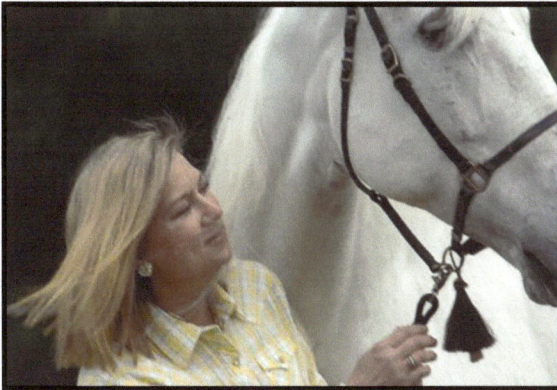

Julie Dillon

A Primer for the Gaited Horse and River
Copyright 2017 by Julie Dillon

This book is dedicated to our Gaited Horses
And those that Love them.

www.horsefeathersnh.com

ISBN: 978-1-944393-42-7
Printed in the United States of America
Cover photos by Vanessa Wright

The thoughts I share in these pages
Reflect what I know today...
. . . More than yesterday,
And if I do it right,
Far less than tomorrow

Acknowledgments

This book is a limited edition. What Gary Lane calls "chips and salsa". There will be another soon with "at least one hundred more" pages.

So I want to especially thank my friend and mentor Gary Lane for lovingly pushing me to do more, be more and believe in myself.

Loren Stevens is the busiest lady I know so I am eternally grateful for the time and amazing talent she invested in proofing and editing.

Deb Putnam is my Equine Industry Guru. Her big picture perspectives helped keep the scope of the work just right.

I also want to thank all my friends and students (many of which are one and the same) for their input and encouragement during the painful proof reading process.

The greatest blessing in life is my husband Matthew. He has bestowed to me his unending love and support in keeping our meadows filled with beautiful horses to love and enjoy.

Introduction

My obsession with and love for horses is congenital. My first word was "Horse". From the first moment of consciousness, I knew I would not be complete without finding my way to a life with horses. As some rock stars have said "I was born this way!".

My parents were bewildered and remained as such throughout my life. Needless to say, growing up in the saddle was not part of my journey. Unlike so many of our great horse masters of today who spent their childhood years on a horse riding stirrup to stirrup with their families and instructors, I took my first formal riding lesson at thirty.

At the age of nineteen, I was able to purchase a horse of my own. He was a dream come true... a pretty grey gelding, perfect in every way. 'Rebel' was the first of many wonderful horses that I have been privileged to have come into my life. Each horse I have been fortunate to know has generously and patiently taught me how much I have to learn. That includes the horses in my life today.

This book is for anyone who thinks they are a "Late Bloomer" as a horseman. I certainly feel that way. And so I have collected these observations for those that may not have started riding as children but began their lessons as purposeful and dedicated adults.

The truth is I cried as I rode my horse home from that first lesson back in '86. The experience was life changing in that the instructor was not so kind and gentle in her evaluation of me as my horses had been. By the time the lesson was over I felt about an inch tall.

It never occurred to me that day that I would ever be an instructor. Even today, each time I give a lesson, my goal is to highlight what folks have accomplished, establish goals for tomorrow and inspire them to know there's nothing they can't do.

This is a collection of some of the fundamental lessons that I would have wanted to learn on that first day as an adult student of horsemanship. I hope you will enjoy my message and perhaps learn a thing or two to help bring you closer to your goals. Try not to get in a hurry...always strive to be as patient and kind to yourself as you would to your horse!

Late Bloomers Are <u>Still</u> Bloomers

"Footsteps of Grey John" 10yo TWH G

Gait: The order in which the horse moves his feet.

"A Gaited Horse is a horse that moves with at least one foot on the ground at all times."

Few people ever forget their first experience riding a gaited horse. It is truly delightful and relaxing to enjoy the beauty of the countryside from the back of any fine horse. But the smooth way of going of the gaited breeds allows us the ability to ride all day and dance all night.

As an instructor, it is a special treat to put folks

3

new to gaited horses on their first gaited lesson master! It is a pleasure to see the smile and incredulously joyful expression dance across their faces. There is a remarkable difference between riding a trot and a well-timed four beat gait!

Once you decide to purchase a gaited horse, it is very important to take the time to go out and ride several different breeds. For your safety, be sure to ride only properly trained and well-gaited horses. A good way to do this is to take lessons from a Certified Riding Instructor on a well trained gaited "Lesson Master". A finished horse that is trained to accept a beginner rider is called a "Lesson Master."

It is important for you to gain the knowledge and body memory of the basic gaits. This will enable you to make an informed decision about what gait is best for you and your body type.

In your research, you may find you prefer one type of four beat gait and breed over another. It will be a great advantage for you to understand what is comfortable for you as you begin shopping for your first or next gaited horse to enjoy. Later, we will talk about some critical points and guidelines for safety during the selection and purchasing process.

"The best way to __find__ a well Gaited Horse is to know what it feels to __ride__ a well Gaited Horse!"

The fellow I married is nothing like mom and dad. When we met, I had been a horse owner for many years so he knew what he was in for. It did take a while for him to realize that my passion and daily requirement for these beautiful creatures would dictate his entire lifestyle. I think I was about forty-two

4

when he realized I wasn't going to outgrow them.

For the first several years of our marriage my husband's work moved us around. Having a horse of my own didn't fit into our budget. During this time, I found many opportunities to work with and ride other folk's horses. While their owners were working forty to sixty hours a week most horses needed a few extra hours of attention to keep them honest. I was more than happy to groom, ride and polish up their horse's training and manners so both horses and riders would be ready for pleasant uneventful weekends on the trail.

When Lauren, our first child, came along Matt bought me a horse of my own. And I loved the precedent! But it wasn't until six years later our second baby, Erin, arrived that Matt gave me a little white horse named "GoBoy."

Matt Dillon, Equine Enabler with the HorseFeathers Boys

I had been riding stock type horses for over thirty years so I didn't know "GoBoy" was gaited or that "smooth gaited" horses even existed. But the way he moved was exhilarating! A knowledgeable horse woman named Tracy Francis was a fellow boarder at the place where I kept my horses. She was experienced with the Saddlebred and Walking Horse breeds and generously shared her knowledge with me. Those "tall grass" lessons with Tracy were the just the beginning of my unending education on what it takes to keep these horses gliding in rhythm.

The Walking Horse

The Tennessee Walking Horse (TWH) became a recognized breed in 1935. Up until then these horses had been in development for at least a hundred years. They originated in middle Tennessee and were bred of Narragansett and Canadian Pacer, Standardbred, Thoroughbred, Morgan and American Saddlebred Stock.

Today's Walking Horses do a wide spectrum of different gaits. Walking Horses also vary greatly in size and shape depending on their bloodlines and how their natural confirmation is developed. The method implemented to "back" or train a horse to the saddle critically influences the ability and appearance of any horse.

Not surprising, it is those training principals that develop the horse's topline and core muscles that give him a greater ability to carry a rider. They also make the horse more relaxed, confident and capable.

This is especially true of our gaited Horses in that they are born and bred to have rhythm right out of the oven!

Only when they are trained to carry weight by a capable and patient hand can they perform their signature movements under saddle with a rider. The Walking Horse's signature gait is the **Flat Walk** which is an extended version of the regular walk.

The **Regular Walk** is a **Lateral Gait**. Lateral Gait refers to the way weight is transferred from the horse's back leg to front leg on each side. Example: left hind, left fore, right hind, right fore. The hoof lands flat onto the ground in four clear even beats.

This is what every horse gaited or non-gaited typically does when headed home after a relaxing trail ride: long, low, four beat with lateral pairs making a "V" on each side. The hind hooves land under the weight bearing area just behind the girth line. The horse transfers his weight to two or three feet on the ground at all times.

*Riding Your Gaited Horse in
Two and Three foot Weight Transference
Builds the Muscle Groups Needed for
Balance and Core Strength*

An upward transition is the action of asking for more impulsion from behind to obtain greater forward movement from the horse.

The upward transition from the Regular Walk for our Walking Horses is the **Flat Walk**. The Flat Walk is a four beat long, low lilting gait that gives the rider a sweeping sensation similar to dancing a waltz. With each step, the horse nods his head in the shape of an "A" in rhythm with his hind feet. The hind legs sweep forward with very little vertical hock action. The horse looks like he is walking in back and "trotting" in front. In an action referred to as **Overstride**, each hind foot "tracks over" that of the correlating lateral front foot. The distance of Overstride will vary with every horse and increase in the upper transitions.

The extension of the Flat Walk is the **Running Walk**. This is a faster, more powerful version of the Flat Walk with more energy and thrust from the hind-quarters. The footfall sequence and weight trans-ference does not change. The horse looks like he is walking in back and "running" in front with very little vertical hock action. Overstride distance increases and the head nod becomes more dynamic in sync with the increased reach and tempo of this beautiful movement.

Patient schooling and lateral exercises executed at a rhythmic Regular Walk builds the horse's abil-ity to do a balanced flowing Flat Walk. And by the same logic, to develop a correct Running Walk, hors-es must first build core and topline musculature at the Flat Walk.

When performing the transitions from the Regular Walk to the Flat Walk and the Flat Walk to the Run-ning Walk, ride your horse softly with light contact in the bridle. Allow and encourage him to maintain his four-beat footfall and two-three foot weight bearing sequence at every speed.

The amount of overstride, natural animation and the depth of the head nod varies with every ani-mal. These are elements of the smooth gaits and the amount displayed by each horse will change depending on his fitness, comfort and sometimes the speed and direction of the wind in the trees.

Gait Chart for Flat Walk and Running Walk   ▶ Weight Bearing Foot   D Lifted Foot

1		2		3		4		5		6		7		8	
▶	▶	▶	▶	▶	▶	D	▶	D	▶	D	D	▶	D	▶	D
D	▶	D	D	▶	D	▶	D	▶	▶	▶	▶	▶	▶	D	▶

The Rack

The Rack is an even four beat lateral gait with a one and two foot weight bearing sequence. Many breed associations have chosen this gait as their signature breed standard footfall. The footfall of the Rack and the Flatwalk is the same except that the horse is moving slower with his front legs and faster with his rear legs. The horse loses the head nod when the horse performing the Racking Gait.

I am not a fan due to the single foot phase in the stride of the Rack. The biomechanical strain of having all of the weight of the horse and rider on just one foot is not conducive to the development of the strength and weight bearing capacity of the horse.

Even if your horse is bred and registered from "Racking Bloodlines" he can learn to Flatwalk. This is done by slowing his rear end cadence until you have clear four beat rhythm and the horse begins to nod his head in time with his back feet. As in all things equine, it takes "as long as it takes". Meanwhile, your Racking horse can and will probably favor the gait that comes natural to his genetic makeup.

As his guardian and keeper be aware of what constitutes good and bad muscle development in the horse at the Racking gait.

Gait Chart for Rack

1	2	3	4	5	6	7	8
▶ D	▶ ▶	D ▶	D ▶	D D	D D	D D	▶ D
D D	D D	D D	▶ D	▶ D	▶ ▶	D ▶	D ▶

The Pace

The **Pace** is a two-beat lateral gait wherein both legs on each side of the horse work together with a moment of suspension between the two beats. When pace occurs it means your horse is working beyond his or her capacity to hold a smooth gait.

When in the saddle if it feels like your horse is dropping your weight with a heavy bounce from side to side, left then right, well, that is the infamous Pace. Sometimes your very first indication is that the head stops nodding.

When anxious and or under an unbalanced rider many gaited horses will fall into a hard Pace or a Step-Pace while others may trot. These are called "default gaits."

Most Gaited horses from time to time will go into these "default gaits" for many reasons. As their bodies change and grow during their years of physical maturation gait can fluctuate. Be conservative about the amount of time you spend riding during the formative years. Young horses under five years are still developing muscle and bone and need ample time to reach their full ability before they spend long hours under tack and rider.

For mature horses that have sustained illness or injury resulting in lameness be aware that it may take extensive reconditioning for a horse to return to his smooth way of going.

This unhealthy gait erodes the horse's ability to carry a rider without harming himself. It damages the weight bearing muscle groups and builds the "hollow" core muscles.

The pace feels like riding a box of rocks and it drops the rider's weight onto the horse's back with every step grinding and eroding the weight bearing muscle groups unless the rider begins to post. (If we wanted to post to avoid being smacked up and down in the saddle, we wouldn't be riding gaited horses!) You can probably figure out that this is not good for your back or joints either!

To correct the Pace, it is necessary to slow down and go back to a much slower speed at which the horse's head nod returns and you can once again feel a clear four beat rhythm.

Count to Four...Every Ride, Every Stride!

The Step Pace (Stepping Pace)

Well geeze...this gait is a tough one because it really feels great when some horses are in it. A lot has been written about the Stepping Pace (or Step Pace) and it is a fairly controversial gait. Because only until recently are folks coming to realize this is hollow movement.

The Stepping Pace is a lateral two-beat unevenly timed gait with minimized overstride. Due to the minimized or lack of **Overstride** (which is when the horse is reaching his hind feet well forward and placing them down beyond the track of the lateral fore) this way of going will eventually break down the weight bearing capacity of most horses.

Studies in equine biomechanics have shown that riding the horse consistently at the Stepping Pace over time can actually cause the last rib and the first lumbar tine to impinge. This dynamic of pressure on the horse's back coupled with the "hollow" footfall will eventually lead to permanent unsoundness. This is not a case of "if" it is a case of "when".

The Stepping Pace is difficult to feel in the saddle as it is only a split second off of the even timing of the Flat Walk and it feels a lot like a Rack. Even from the ground it is sometimes hard to see the difference between the Stepping Pace and the Rack. Look for uneven timing, stiffness in the shoulders and notice that both legs on each side of the horse are lifting together. If there is a head nod it is moving in a "V" shaped movement side to side rather than a correct straight "A" pattern.

Some horses will do a Stepping Pace at liberty but the harm occurs when performing this gait under the weight of a rider. This gait erodes the gait-performing and weight bearing muscle groups and strengthens the "hollow" core muscles. Hollow core muscles are those that when strengthened make the horse weaker and less able to carry a rider.

As with the Pace, in order to correct the Stepping Pace slow down and go back to the speed at which the horse's head nod returns and you can once again feel a clear four beat rhythm.

Gait Chart for Pace and Step Pace

1		2		3		4	
D	D	▶	▶	D	D	▶	▶
▶	▶	D	D	▶	▶	D	D

The Missouri Fox Trotting Horse

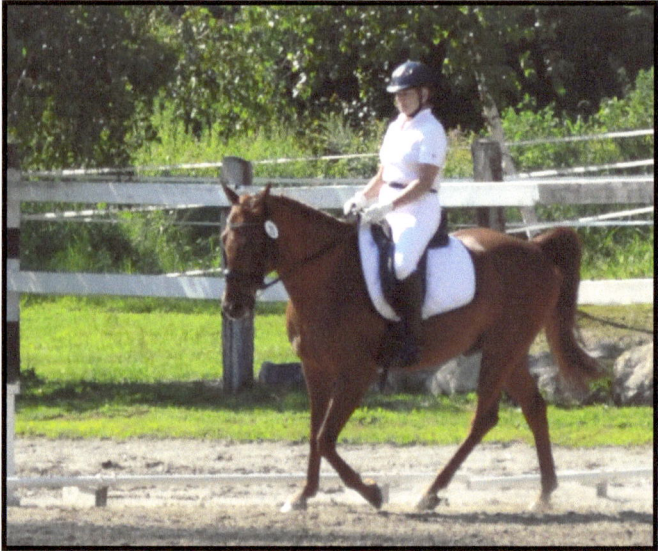

*In a correct Fox Trot there must be
one front foot on the ground at all times.*

Legend has it that over a hundred years ago the folks in Arkansas and Missouri discovered that the Flat Walk gait was not too efficient over the rough terrain of the Ozark Mountain Trails. With the timing of front hooves moving faster than the hind, the horse was often challenged with trying to keep his balance and get out of his own front end while maneuvering over rocks and up and down hills. Not to mention the deep head nod of the Walking Horse made it difficult for the horse to see where he was going!

So from Walking Horse, Morgan, Arabian and other "Pocket" horses (these were gaited bloodlines from private family stock) a new breed of riding horse was borne for the mountain trails.

We have the fine horse breeders of the Ozarks to

thank for the **Fox Trotting Horse** and the signature gait known as the **Fox Trot**. In this unique gait the horse walks with his front legs, trots with his back legs and nods his head in "agreement". The head nod ripples all the way from his nose, over his back and continues down to his "rooster" tail.

The **Fox Trot** is a **Diagonal Gait** and is smooth in a very different way. Some folks often say that it feels like doing the Rumba in the saddle.

This four beat gait is created when the horse transfers his weight from left hind to right fore, then left fore simultaneously with the right hind. (The diagonal fore takes the weight from the hind a split second before the lateral fore hits the ground.)

When performing the Fox Trot, it appears that the horse is trotting behind and walking in front. As with the Flat Walk, when correctly performed the Fox Trot has a two-three foot weight bearing sequence throughout each stride. His hind legs move up and down while his front legs work in a sweeping motion in a back ward striding motion as they come together laterally making a "V" on each side.

In recent years a gait called the "Slick Trot" has been seen and rewarded in some of the gaited show classes. To create this exaggerated gait, the horse is ridden forward onto his forehand. This increases the timing of the front feet and results in a split second of "Fly Time". The "Slick Trot" is an artificial move-ment and does not constitute a smooth way of going, it rides like a box of rocks, and is not correct breed standard.

The Flat Walk is also a correct gait for the Missou-ri Fox Trotting Horse. When showing in rail classes, the Fox Trotting Horse is required to enter at the Flat Walk then move up to the Fox Trot.

I have seen many Missouri Fox Trotting Horses

that could perform the Flat Walk and Running Walk as well as their Walking Horse cousins!

Gait Chart for Foxtrot

1		2		3		4		5		6		7		8	
♪	D	♪	♪	♪	♪	♪	♪	D	♪	D	♪	D	D	♪	D
D	♪	D	♪	D	D	♪	D	♪	D	♪	♪	♪	♪	♪	♪

Why do "Gaited" Horses 'Gait'?
The Gait Keeper Gene

Gaited horses have existed for twenty-two million years! In Tanzania fossil footprints of three Hipparion horses were discovered. The imprinted stride pattern was found to be in the footfall sequence of a running walk at a speed of about nine miles an hour!

As to the "why" of it all, for over a hundred years breeders and trainers of gaited horse have suspected that these horses were fundamentally different but had no proof other than breeding records.

In 2012, the scientific evidence was provided by a team of Swedish researchers at Uppsala University who isolated a protein called **DRMT3**. In gaited horses this protein is stunted and as a result, the spinal cord becomes more flexible. This increased flexibility in the spine leads to a change in coordination associated with lateral locomotion commonly referred to as "Pace".

One study showed that the animals with this genetic code had particular incoordination of limbs and difficulty in running at higher speeds. The "loss of canter" aspect also rings true to logic as many of our "Pacey" gaited horses do have a tough time learning to canter on command.

The Stichting International Foundation for Animal Genetics did a worldwide study of the distribution of the "Gaitkeeper" mutation and found that among the four thousand horses tested, all of the Missouri Fox Trotting Horses, Peruvian Paso Horses, Rocky Mountain Horses and Tennessee Walking Horses had 100% of the DMRT3 factor. Other Paso breeds had more than 95% and the Kentucky Mountain Spotted Horse had 92%. All Standardbred Pacers scored 100% and Standardbred Trotters came in at 97%.

At this writing, you can even have your horse tested for purity of his "Gaited Gene". The University of California Davis now offers a diagnostic test for the 'Genetic A' variant of DMRT3. They will need twenty to thirty hairs with roots to perform the test. Trademarked as "SynchroGait", you can get this done for around $350 per animal.

"Footsteps of Grey John" 14 yo TWH Gelding

The Canter

Yes, both the Walking horse and Missouri Fox Trotting Horse perform a classic three-beat canter with a gliding sensation often called "The Rocking Chair Canter".

As in all breeds the gaited horse's canter footfall are outside hind, inside hind/outside fore, inside fore and a moment of suspension.

The timing of the request should be after the inside hind leg lifts and before the outside hind strikes the ground.

A word of caution: The canter depart from a Flatwalk or Regular Walk is the only fair and acceptable request when asking your gaited horse to canter.

In the most cases, while performing the Running

Walk, the Tennessee Walking Horse's front legs are moving too fast and the knee action is too high to safely perform the upward transition to the canter. Therefore, slow your Walking Horse to the Flat Walk or Regular Walk when asking for the canter.

In the case of the Foxtrotting Horse it is the same. The Fox Trot is a gait wherein the front legs are going slower than the hind (much like that of the extended trot of his non-gaited cousins). To be fair and correct the transition should be requested from the slower gait.

To execute a proper upward transition to the canter the Walking Horse and the Fox Trotting Horse must be performing the Flat Walk, Regular and/or in the case of upper schooling the Collected Walk.

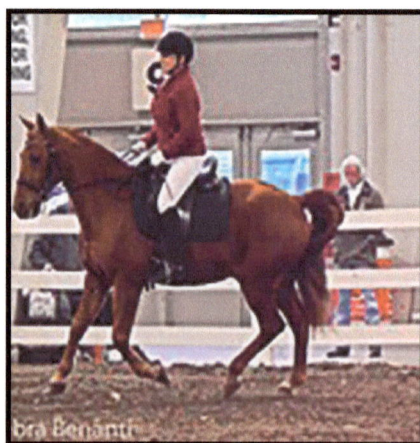

bra Benanti

"Music" TWH G - 19yo
(rider's leg is too far forward)

Keeping your Gaited Horse "Gaited"

Gaited Equitation means to ride four-beat footfall
<u>Every Ride, Every Stride</u>!

In the saddle, take responsibility for your weight and balance by using your core to communicate with your horse.

The best riders do so by "doing nothing at all"

The earliest surviving manuals of horsemanship were written during the time of Socrates by an Athenian Roman Calvary Master named Xenophon. He instructed and trained his mounted officers with same principles that remain the foundation of classic horsemanship today. Xenophon taught us that: "A man shall ride as he walks!"

Which means that every movement you make from the saddle should be the no different than if you were walking on the ground. In order for your horse to remain balanced under your weight, you must maintain your balance over his center of gravity.

Your upper body must stay poised and in a position where you are neither ahead nor behind the motion of the horse. Your legs and seat must be relaxed and in correct placement to keep your core in the middle of the horse taking care to stay centered (neither left nor right) of the horse's midline.

Let your bones do their job by sitting up with the type of posture required to balance a book upon your head. Your ribcage must be lifted over your pelvis and your shoulders in alignment with your hips. Elbows must drop directly below your shoulder sockets. And your ears must be in line with your heels, hips, elbow and shoulders.

Learning to maintain your core balance will not only improve your horsemanship, it will also go a long way to keeping you moving in youthful balance on the ground well into your golden years.

"Show me your horse and I'll tell you who you are."
An English Proverb

Our horses will tell on us in a very intimate way. They feel every imbalance in our body. If you have as much as a sore toe your horse will feel you compensate in some way to relieve the pressure on that area. The horse will either reward or "rat you out" on your riding skills as well! So be aware that if you are inconsistent in your aids because so will your horse be inconsistent in response.

Sit in the saddle as though you are walking with a book on top of your head, then without changing this posture, relax your upper body completely. Let your elbows drop from your shoulder sockets and bring your forearms up from your sides to point directly to the ring in the bit. Hold your hands closed with your thumbs up.

If during your ride things are not going quite right, look to your part of the equation. When you are not getting the response from your horse you want or need check the pressure in your stirrups, seat bones, legs, and the length of your reins for equal balance and measure. Is your bridle adjusted to the same length on each side? There have been times when I have had someone borrow and re-adjust a bridle or an off-billet strap on my saddle. Always check your tack and girth for fit and safety before mounting up so that "Operator Errors" of that nature can be avoided.

Once you are mounted, check your body position when in the saddle. Make sure you have equal distribution of body weight in your seat, legs, and stirrups. Maintain a balanced upright but relaxed position in the saddle. Symmetrical use of your weight and balance will allow you to more consistently use the same leg and seat pressure each time you ride. If it is necessary to use strong leg signals in the beginning, lighten the intensity of your movements over time as the horse progresses.

Gradually lighten your movements and the connection between you and your horse will become a silent, seamless joy to experience and for others to behold.

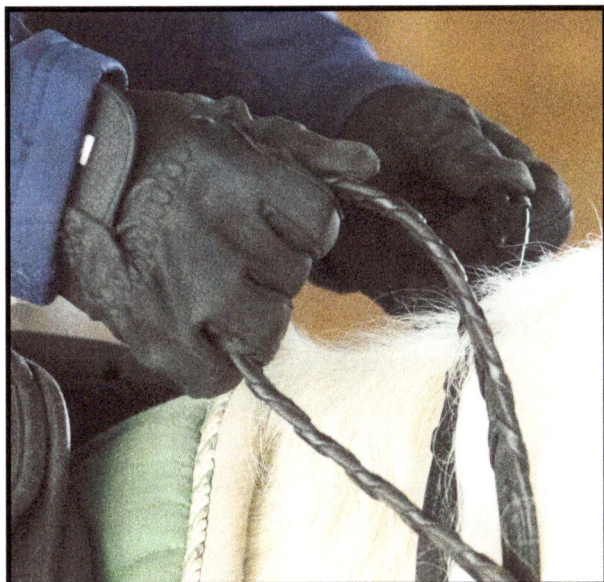

Rein aids to encourage Consistent Gait

Take a "contact" rein position in order to have your rein aids work independently with each other as well as with your seat and legs. Contact reining allows you to give a signal to each side of the bit and allows independent movement between your hands. Take a rein in each hand closed firmly between your bottom two fingers. The remainder of the reins (called the "bight") goes out of your palm between your thumb and "pointer" finger.

Think "in through the bottom fingers and out through the top" with firm contact. The loop in the reins should lie under the right rein between the rein and the horse's neck.

Allow just enough equal length in the both reins to create a straight line from your elbow to the ring in the bit. The length and tension on the rein is correct when you can move just your bottom two fingers in a "check and release" action on the bit.

The "release" should always be a slightly larger movement and enough to encourage forward movement while the "check" action strong enough to signal the horse to slow down and encourage him to rock his weight back onto his hind end.

Always follow a "checking" rein action immediately with a "release" rein action. In this way, you are rewarding the horse for responding to your request. It is the first indication to the horse that he has done well. As soon as he begins to understand what you want, your horse will begin enjoy the learning process. As your horse becomes more sensitive to contact reining, this check and release action should soften to the point that the bit just gently massages the bars of the horse's mouth.

Gait and collection begins from behind! Yours and your horse's. Your seat, weight and leg control the horse's movement. Once you obtain forward movement, rein aids tell him where to put his nose and how to use his neck, shoulder and front end.

Ride from back to front, relax your lumbar region and allow your hips to individually follow the motion of your horse's hind legs. Sometimes this takes some getting used to and you will need to relax your lower back to let each of side of your pelvis to be independently lifted, advanced and rolled forward with each step of the horse's hind legs.

This way you can begin to his feel gait and footfall sequence as your body moves with his. Now when you are ready you can begin to set his cadence and timing by slowing down or speeding up your hip bones.

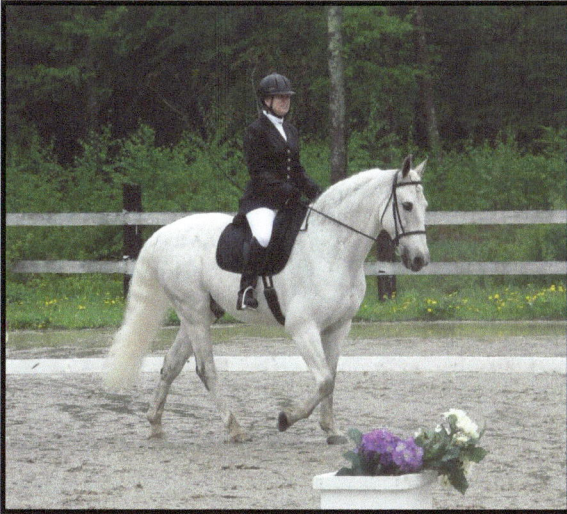

Putting it all together: How Core, Leg and Rein Cues work together to encourage four beat gait and cadence.

To encourage and support your horse in his gait, combine light pressure from your legs with a correlating cues from diagonal rein pressure. By using these diagonal aids you can control your horse's speed and footfall cadence.

Diagonal means "opposite corners". **Diagonal aids** combine the use of your left contact rein with your right leg and your right contact rein with your left leg.

To maintain a four beat way of going, ease your weight gently into one side of your seat bones and apply just the weight of one lower leg onto the horse's opposite side. Use pressure from your diagonal leg on one side to encourage forward movement, then gently check and release the opposite rein. Repeat these diagonal aids in a one-two-three-four beat cadence to create a four-beat signal from your seat, leg and reins.

Start slowly; do not ask for speed until he maintains a forward, smooth, even four-beat cadence. Later, this method can be used to adjust the speed and timing of any gait.

Purposeful intent: Always be clear and consistent in your message. Repeat as many times as it takes but keep the new lessons no longer than ten minutes at a time, then move on to a familiar task that the horse does well.

Patience: This is the one element you cannot do without when dealing with your horse on any level. Begin by warming him up at a regular walk to assure he is ready mentally and physically. Any time you are teaching your horse something new, have a definite goal in mind. Start by asking for what the horse already knows how to do. Keep new lessons to about ten minutes at a time and be sure to finish the schooling session with a favorite activity he enjoys and does well so that you always end on a positive note.

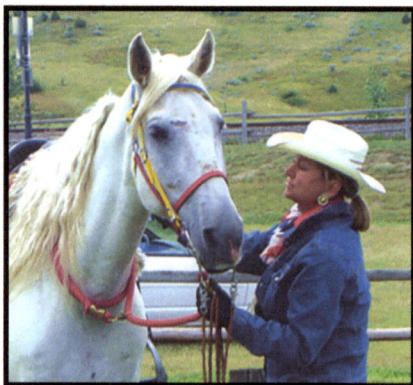

" Julie, the only three things you need to train your horse are: Patience, Patience, and Patience."

As told to me by Mark Russell.

Give the horse plenty of time to think the lesson through (he gets it when he gets it).

Are you asking the right question? Are you using the proper aids to correctly ask? Be sure you are asking in a way the horse can understand.

Do you know the answer? Be sure you know when to release and reward your horse when teaching him something new. And the reward should include time for the horse to think it through and retain the lesson.

Reward, Reward, Reward: Be ready to acknowledge and praise your horse for the smallest effort toward the proper answer. Let the horse know when he does it right. If he is not getting it, ignore and forgive what he does "wrong". Check your delivery of the lesson and your methods.

Study, Ride, Study, Ride: There are many masters of equitation both ancient and current, English and Western. Start your library of favorites whether it be in book or DVD form.

Spend some of your down time building your knowledge of horsemanship from clinicians that share your way of thinking about things. What you may find is that the advice and wisdom of these great educators will affirm those things that you know and do well and perhaps encourage you to learn more. Just ten minutes of reading can give you enough inspiration for hours of thought and application in the saddle.

Selecting an Instructor: The riding instructor's greatest responsibility is your safety. He or she should be dedicated to keeping you in the saddle on a worthy and well matched horse.

If you have a training problem it should be their mission to help you find the best trainer available to work with you and your horse. A good instructor should not be afraid to advise you accordingly if your horse is not a good match. Most reliable and certified instructors have a network of associates that can be called in for consultation on just about any training issue.

If your Instructor doesn't have an Instructor you are drinking from a stagnant pond.

Select a dedicated learner to take your lessons from. The study of horsemanship is an endless journey and joyful way to spend a lifetime. I take lessons on a regular basis to be sure to serve my students to the best of my ability. My instructor has more than one instructor and they all take lessons!

Find someone you don't mind sitting down to dinner with. If they make you feel capable of anything, they are probably a good choice.

The instruction that you take should serve the goals you have in mind for you and your horse. There are many enjoyable trail and arena disciplines in which to participate in that serve to build the bond between horse and rider. Every discipline has folks that specialize in teaching the basics and refined training for participating and enjoying playdays, trail rides, competitions and shows.

Gait Improvement with Classical Training

There has never been a better time than now to learn about being a responsible partner in movement with your horse. In today's equine culture there is a renewal of the study of Classical Training across multiple disciplines. Our Gaited Clinicians and Trainers across the country are teaching folks a more patient, systematic and fair process of training the horse.

Each time we mount up, we must ask the horse to move correctly so that he becomes ever stronger and more capable of carrying weight.

A major component of Classical Training is the use of **Lateral Exercises**. These exercises help the horse build his topline strength and therefore more easily bear the weight of a rider. Learning to ask your horse to do these simple movements will help him learn to leverage his strength and carrying power from back to front.

Lateral exercises strengthen the horse's weight-bearing muscle groups by teaching him to engage his hindquarters, elevate his back and lighten his forehand.

It is very important that we teach the horse to use his body in this way so that when we ask them to carry us we do no harm.

The fair way to introduce lateral work is to teach them from the ground before asking your horse to do these movements under saddle.

Begin teaching your horse suppling exercises in hand at a very slow walk. Start along the rail using your outside rein to guide the horse while lightly cueing him forward at the girth line as illustrated (here I use a long "impulsion wand"). Measure your steps to match the stride and reach of his front legs with yours. Think "forward, straight and calm". Take as much time as you and your horse needs to settle into a rhythm.

Introduce Lateral Movement on the Ground

Once you have gotten the horse accustomed to following your aids in a straight line, begin asking him to move in an outward spiral. Keep the horse's bend from nose to tail aligned with the arc of the increasing spiral. Ask for the spiral out in both directions and then begin the exercise in the saddle.

On days when you are unable to ride, these in-hand exercises are a great way to spend quality productive time with your horse. As you perfect the spiral-in-and spiral-out movements, you may want to leg yield and later the shoulder-in.

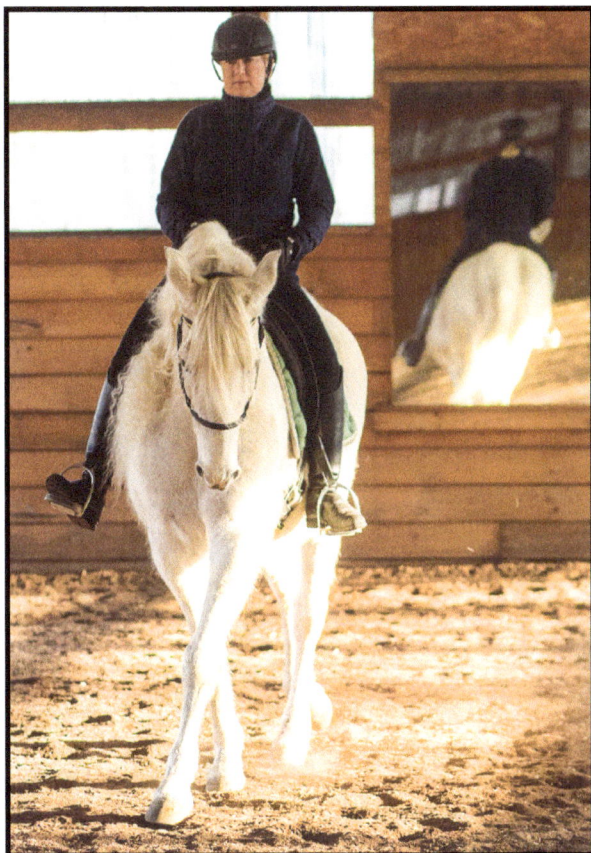

'Sterling' demonstrating the Leg Yield

It is a fact that the **Shoulder-In** exercise breaks up the hard pace into a walk or flat walk. It is physically very difficult for a horse to pace if he is moving on three tracks in the bend of a spiral, circle or along a wall.

The "Cowboy Shoulder-In" is a simple, easy way to supple the muscles of each side of your horse. Start in the middle of an imaginary circle and ride your horse at a relaxed walk in an outward spiral. Increase the size of the circle about twelve to eighteen inches with each rotation.

It is important that the horse remain on the bend from nose to tail during these exercises. The inside hind foot should reach under the midline in rhythm with the outside fore. Continue to spiral-out pattern at the walk in each direction, then start outward and spiral-in toward the middle of the circle. Keep it slow and in four beat timing. You will be amazed at how this one exercise improves your Gaited Horse's ability and strength to get and maintain four beat way of going!

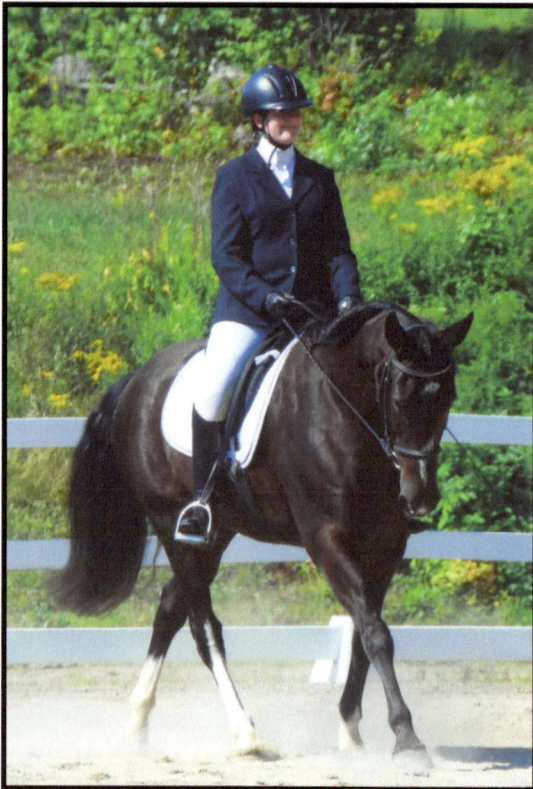

Aceman & Molly White on 20 Meter Circle

Selecting Your First or Next Gaited Horse
Look for Mature, Talented, Finished

An adult horse with several years under saddle that is "set" in his gaits is a better choice and a much smoother beginning for the rider just discovering the easy-gaited breeds. Do consider purchasing a sound horse in good health in his teenage years. Older horses can often be more forgiving and can provide years of pleasurable companionship on the trail as well as an easy introduction to easy gaited riding. Many times the horse that has been well cared for by a single owner over a long period of time is a good prospect.

It is the rare five year old horse of any breed that is perfectly set in his gaits and timing. If this is your very first gaited experience, insist on a horse that does not require daily schooling to maintain gait.

Most unfinished gaited horses (just as with non-gaited horses) require the skills of a trainer to develop and keep them in proper cadence. It can take years of consistent training for a horse to develop the muscle groups to maintain gait under a rider's weight.

That said, if you have a talent for training young horses and are up to the challenge, starting a gaited prospect is much the same as training a horse that trots. The gaited youngsters require the same amount of patience, skill and sensitive application of correct aids as any other horse.

Number one rule when riding horses in any situation:

NEVER GET ON A HORSE YOU HAVE NOT SEEN SOMEONE ELSE RIDE SUCCESSFULLY!

If the seller won't or can't ride him, why should you risk it?!

"He's gaited . . . but he's still a Horse!"

Some General Rules That Apply to All Horse Purchases

It is an exciting time when you find yourself searching for that perfect trail buddy. Ladies often say it is like looking for the perfect spouse and that's a good way to think about it. Focus on exactly what you want in a horse and stick to your resolve. Patience is your best friend in this journey. It is a difficult road to walk down when all your friends are passing you by at a canter. But, getting back in the saddle also requires keeping yourself safe during the selection process. Hold onto your wits through all the anticipation as you visit farms and barns looking for the perfect horse.

This is worth repeating: If the seller won't ride him or cannot provide a willing individual to ride the horse and demonstrate what the horse can do, my advice is to walk away. And never mind what they say about the horse.

Always think safety first! Life is too short to risk any injury or danger to you or your loved ones while trying to ride a bad or questionable prospect. Resulting injuries could limit your ability to ride and enjoy the company of a good horse.

Even when the seller does ride the horse, **if you don't like what you see or if you just get a creepy feeling about the whole situation, walk away!** And make no apologies!

When you arrive to evaluate a potential new mount, pay close attention to how the seller handles the horse and the way the horse responds.

Ground manners are of utmost importance and lay the foundation for communication under saddle.

For example: if the horse is not respectful and walks all over the current owner, that horse is going think you are a doormat, too. In this case, the horse's former handler has taught him that people are below him on the pecking order. Don't consider a horse of this nature unless you have the skill and desire to re-train him.

Many different cultures exist in the horse world and sometimes the best and most harmonious transfers of ownership occur between buyers and sellers of similar background and practice. In other words, if you are looking for a quiet trail prospect, don't expect to find Mr. Perfect in a barn where Barrel Racing is a regular Saturday night event. But if a Western Trail and Obstacle Course Champion is retired from the show ring and goes up for sale, you may have hit pay dirt.

Registration Papers: All things equal, the registered prospect gets my vote. Papers on a horse can tell you a lot about where he came from and where he's been. It is just like a birth certificate, the horse's birth place, birth date, breeding, the name of the breeder is listed. Usually, each former owner also appears in chronological order allowing you to track and research his foundation bloodlines and subsequent training and experience.

Registered versus Non-Registered

It is true that you "can't ride papers", but if he is registered, take a good look at the papers before you purchase a horse. If they indicate that he has changed owners frequently, it is a good idea to take the time to make some calls to those former owners. Try to learn as much information about the horse as possible to help you with your decision-making process.

You may find that your perfect horse is not registered and that's just fine. Be aware that without "papers" horses are frequently not allowed to compete in certain breed exhibits and shows. However, if you do decide to show your unregistered horse, there are many "open" competitions that include all breeds and multiple disciplines.

The Changing of the Guard

Most of us have enjoyed a relationship with the "Perfect Horse" and then suffered the heartbreak of losing them (mostly from old age). We are well equipped to extend the lives of our beloved horses but so well equipped to deal with the loss of a fine horse after many years or in most cases decades. It is especially difficult to find your next equine companion as the memories of that one amazing horse are still hanging in our thoughts and tugging on the hearstrings.

That is part of the joy and sadness that having horses in our lives brings. The Aceman and I were together for twenty years and every other horse will be measured by his talent, skill, heart and courage in the arena and on the trail.

So in these cases make an effort to be mindfull that the new guy is "not your horse"...not at first anyway. It is best not to compare or have any expectation of a critter until you taken the time to get to know the new recruit and ask what activities best suit his fancy.

One of the best scenarios I have experienced is a case where I met a fantastic horse and shyly asked the owner to please advise me if she ever decided to convey him. To my great fortune, two years later the owner called! He is nothing like the "Aceman" but little "Jesse" has carved a place of his own in my life and my heart.

Yes, there is room in your life for more than one great horse!

Photo by Vanessa Wright

Other things to consider when looking to buy a horse

• **Temperament, Talent, and Training** should be considered top priorities.

• "**Pretty is as Pretty does!**" If you fall in love with a pretty face that may be all you wind up with.

• Don't show up to look at a new horse for the first time with an empty trailer.

• Pre-purchase Veterinary Exams are worth every penny and can save you big bucks down the line.

• Horses live a long time and are expensive to maintain so buy as perfect a match to your needs as you can find.

• "**Green and Green makes Black and Blue.**" If you are new to horses, purchase an older, well trained horse. Youngsters are best left to seasoned, experienced horsemen.

• "**It's easier to buy than it is to sell.**"

Bringing Your New Horse Home
Methods for a Safe and Happy Transition

When a new horses arrive, it is a huge event for our farm and we treat them like a new puppy. We make a huge "fuss" over them and spend hours reassuring them that this is their new home and we are over the moon about them joining the family. It is a bit mushy and maybe not for everyone. But within a few days they settle in and begin to appreciate the routine of their new environment.

There is an old time philosophy that says, "Throw them in . . . let 'em sink or swim!". But, if you value the safety and usefulness of your animals, this may not be for you. Time and patience can reduce the chance of the heartache and aggravation of changing bandages instead of saddle pads.

Position the new guy in a stall or paddock where he can get a chance to see but not touch his new stable mates.

This is the most exciting time for every owner: bringing your new horse home! The searching, selecting and the purchasing process is often exhausting and time consuming. Now your decision is made and the deal is finalized. In order to be able to enjoy your new acquisition, you must keep the newcomer safe in his new environment while the settling-in period passes.

There is usually not much to be concerned about if your barn has separate stalls and runs for each animal. As long as the horse gets frequent socialization from you and his other caregivers, this is the most ideal environment for an incident-free homecoming. Some horses settle in like they have been there all their lives, however, others need frequent reassurance and positive distractions.

Most equine setups require that horses be turned out for liberty in groups. Integrating a new member into this delicate social structure requires careful planning and consideration. If done too quickly, chances are high your vet will ultimately become involved.

Assuming that you are thoroughly familiar with your horses at home (and also that you are an "Alpha owner"), this process should be given a period of two to four weeks to complete. In some cases when dealing with strong personalities, a longer period may be necessary.

For a few days at a time allow each herd member introduction across the fence. Begin with your most docile personality and then work up to your Alpha horse.

The Alpha horse is the one who calls the shots, keeps the herd together and tells each horse when and where to graze.

It is helpful and often crucial to know from the former owner what position your new horse held or if he ran in a group before his arrival. Also get as much detail as possible about his habits and attitudes toward other herd members. By cycling each of your existing herd members next to him, you will get an indication as to what combination of horses poses a risk of injury.

After two or three weeks (there really is no set time) select the first turnout partner according to the most friendly exchange among the new acquaintances.

When putting new acquaintances together select a time when you can be there to keep watch over the new relationship in the event the horses may need to be separated.

During the first several days, give them as much time as possible together but always under supervision. Be ready to intervene if a violent confrontation begins. If after three or four days of uneventful supervised turnout, you are most likely safe in assuming that your herd integration is well underway.

Continue to introduce each new personality up through the "seniority" levels. And always be there for the first few days to guard a new situation. This method gives your new horse time to find his place in the pecking order slowly and can reduce the opportunity for costly injuries.

Once your new horse is integrated fully into the existing herd, be sure feeding time is handled safely. At feeding time, always separate your horses in areas where they can eat undisturbed. Removing hunger and competition for food as a motivation for a fight greatly increases the level of contentment among herd members.

Individual stalls are best for meals where grain and supplements are dispensed, but often it is necessary to feed hay out in a pasture to a group of horses. If so, make certain there is always an extra feeding and that the hay piles are spaced well apart.

Example: If you are feeding hay in a large open area to three horses, be sure that four piles of hay feedings are made available. Space them a good distance apart. No individual should have to worry about "poachers" on the attack before he has had an opportunity to finish his meal.

Should the Alpha horse decide that one feeding looks better than the others and the entire herd shifts, there is always an open meal for the guy at the bottom of the pecking order. Some of these aggressive individuals are perpetual bullies and refuse to yield to any other Alpha personality. They are not to be trusted with milder mannered horses.

Often, the resulting veterinary care costs involved with keeping aggressive horses pastured with the rest of the herd is more than the expense of fencing necessary to keep them apart.

Signs of abuse such as missing patches of fur or bite marks on your more easy going members of the herd should be watched for at all times. Lower ranked horses really benefit from a break from time to time. Two or three times a week give them liberty time without the Alpha individual.

This also helps if you are working on social issues such as a horse balking at leaving the barn under saddle without a stable mate ("herd-bound"). Giving these horses individual time in the pasture can ease the pattern of dependency that leaves them feeling insecure about venturing out alone.

There are gender specific issues to be considered. Many facilities save themselves a lot of headaches by making it a policy that mares and geldings are turned out separately. Even though castrated, geldings will challenge each other over control of a mare. Additionally, Alpha mares have been known to do serious damage to a bossy and overbearing gelding.

Not always but often, one mare in a group of geldings can cause utter chaos and create conflict unending. Not unlike some human social gatherings I have observed.

These are just a few guidelines that can help with this weighty and important task. Decide what works for you among the information offered here.

The best way to keep your horses safe from each other is to develop an awareness of the habits of your horses at home and take time to get to know your new arrival before deciding your course of action.

Without fail, every time I have cut corners and rushed this process, it has cost me valuable time in the saddle.

Other Considerations: Teeth & Feet

Relaxation is the key to allowing the horse to comfortably move the way nature intended. Nature intended for your gaited horse to move smoothly by transferring his weight to the foot or feet on the ground. Here are some elements that can interfere with his comfort, relaxation and smooth way of going:

Proper care of his **Feet and Teeth** make or break a horse's ability and attitude. Regular maintenance in these two areas is essential. If his teeth hurt or his feet are improperly cared for your horse cannot even pay attention to what you are asking him. Sudden negative changes in behavior are often caused by problems in these two areas.

Floating teeth once or twice a year is important and will keep your horse "happy in the bridle". He will also be better able to chew his food, less likely to drop grain while eating and more likely to stay in good weight.

Gaited horses have a very strong hoof wall and most can do well without shoes. There is a recognized standard for trimming a gaited horse to help and encourage with a desired way of going.

As a general rule: A longer toe and shorter heel will give more lift. A shorter toe and higher heel will give more reach. Example: If you have a "pacey" horse, then you want a long toe in front and a shorter toe with more heel in back. For a "trotty" horse, you want a shorter toe in the front to break off the ground faster and longer toe in back.

This is just a very basic overview of gaited trimming principals. Find a Farrier in your area that understands the gaited breeds and is good with your horses. Consult that specialist for further detailed information. Gaited horses do not need shoes to have a smooth way of going but just like with any other horse, most need protective shoeing or footwear if ridden on hard or rocky surfaces.

It is a good policy to have your Equine Dentist and a well-qualified Farrier out on a regular schedule, it's just good horsemanship: proper care, custody and control saves a lot of headaches.

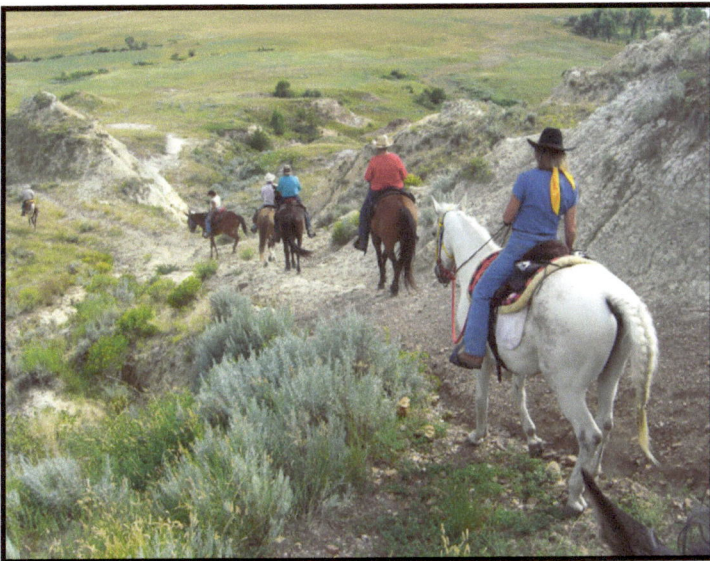

The first morning of an all-day trail ride is a bad time to see if your horse will tolerate a new bit.

Bits & Saddles

Bits and Bitting: When working with a new horse, if you like his way of going, don't change the bit. If you decide to go to a different bit, make sure you have an academic understanding of how it works and know how to use it properly. For your safety, make any major tack changes in an enclosed area over time to be sure that you have good control before going out on the trail.

Most older gaited horses you will find today have been trained on a shank and curb bit. It could be dangerous to ride these horses in a snaffle or lesser piece of equipment without thorough retraining. Some folks have drastically changed from shank to snaffle with disastrous results. Be aware that it takes years of gradual schooling to train a horse to respect a loose ring snaffle when he is accustomed to a long shank bit with a curb strap. Your safety and continued health is the most important thing above all else!

The good news is that currently our master horse trainers are starting our gaited youngsters in a plain snaffle bit using the "less is more" classical training methods.

Saddle Fit can allow flow of or restrict movement. Saddle design must allow for the horse to have full extension and reach in his shoulder and scapula. The saddle should lie level without "bridging" along the horse's back. The front of the saddle fit between the area just behind the scapula and in front of the last rib.

Proper placement of the girth can be measure at around four inches behind the elbow of the horse's front leg.

Look for a saddle that is a "balanced" seat. This means that it is designed with the stirrup attachment in a location that places your leg in line with the rest your body as you sit in the saddle. Good equitation is made easier with equipment that helps you keep your "heel-hip-shoulder-ear" position without tension or reaching to maintain proper alignment. These saddles allow your body to easily and softly align in a balanced position.

With so many styles and brands available, it is often a long, arduous trial of trying, buying and re-selling several models before you find just the best brand and fit for you and your horse.

Proper distribution of your weight and balance is crucial to good horsemanship. As you gain increasing control in the saddle, these elements become natural aids in directing the flow of or restricting movement while riding your horse.

If you are buying a new horse that is gaiting well under a particular saddle and you find that it is also a good fit for you, don't hesitate to offer to purchase the saddle in the deal.

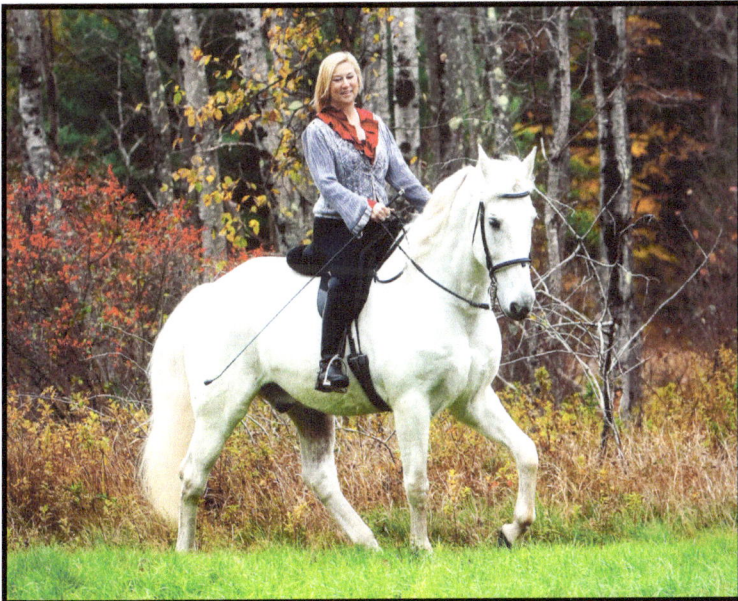

Dressage Training for Gaited Horses

Gaited Dressage was once considered an unlikely phrase. Today, this comprehensive learning process for our gaited horses and those that love them is spreading across the nation.

From the sidelines unless you have done some study and mounted practice a dressage test can look like watching paint dry. However, this purposeful and sequential form of horse training is beneficial to participants and spectators alike.

What I have learned is that Dressage shows are not about earning first place in the traditional sense wherein your goal is to win a blue ribbon. The Dressage test is actually an opportunity to measure your progress in what you have accomplish in the training of your horse. Dressage students attend shows to understand how well they are following the requirements of the training scale for the good of the horse.

The training scale is a progressive guide for the rider to learn to develop a forward, relaxed, physically strong, and mentally capable equine partner in movement.

The tests riders execute in the Dressage arena are a set of movements designed to measure the percentage of "correctness" you have achieved with the work you have done to train your horse. United States Dressage Federation (USDF) and United States Equestrian Federation (USEF) judges study for many years to hold a seat in the booth at a Dressage Competition. They are also first and foremost educators dedicated to the instruction of the training of horse and rider.

USDF approved tests for our Gaited horses are now available from Intro to Fourth Level at Friends of Sound Horses (www.FOSH.com) and at National Walking Horse Association (www.NWHA.com). The inclusiveness, approval and encouragement of the USDF and USEF Judges toward our efforts has been humbling and affirming. Gaited competitors participating in Open Dressage and Combined Training Shows are doing very well and are also being well received by USEF and USDF accredited judges all over the country!

Rail competitors Train to Show
Dressage competitors Show to Train

Dressage Tests: a brief overview

Each dressage test is a comprehensive exercise designed to develop and measure the level of communication and accuracy between horse and rider. As you work your way up the training scale, the difficulty only slightly increases allowing a gradual progression. Upon close study, they are symmetrical, simple and easy to accomplish with your horse when applied with patience and consideration.

Every four years, the United States Dressage Association releases a new revision of the tests. This keeps the work fresh and everyone on their toes!

Intro: Anyone who has an obedient, forward and willing mount and has ridden down a trail at a walk and flatwalk is qualified to execute an Intro Level Test. Intro A and B focus on walk, intermediate gait, square halt and free walk. Intro C Introduces the Canter depart on the half circle.

Training Level: If you and your horse can canter a circle with quiet aids from and then back down to a flatwalk, you are on your way to Training Level. These tests gently and responsibly introduce the canter and layers it upon the skills gained at Intro Level. The final test requires a stretching exercise at the flatwalk on a twenty meter circle.

First Level: When you are ready to work on strengthening your horse and are testing well at Training Level, it is time to consider moving up. First Level begins Lateral Work: Lengthening of Stride and Leg Yielding. These are suppling exercises that build the top line and abdominal muscles for an ever stronger and more capable horse. Circles tighten from twenty to fifteen meters and the judges look for more "jump" in the canter.

Second Level: Demonstrates that the horse accepts more weight on the hind and displays more thrust at the medium gaits. The study of Leg and Seat aids is further in depth and Second Level requires the Shoulder-In, Travers and Counter-Canter. Here circles decrease from fifteen to ten meters at the canter and departs are from the collected walk rather than the flat walk. Increased emphasis is on bending, suppleness and self-carriage.

Third Level: Third Level combines all of the previous work to ask the horse and rider to now demonstrate each previously practiced Level. The horse must demonstrate the ability to move in medium and extended gaits with clear cadence, distinction and in collection. The flying change of leads is required to graduate to the fourth level.

General Information: Gaited horses are judged by the same standards and elements of the Training Scale as that of trotting horses. The exception: our Intermediate Gait is the Flatwalk for Walking Horses and a slow Foxtrot for Missouri Foxtrotting Horses. As with any type of competition, be sure that your horse is ready and capable of remaining calm while attending a large gathering of people and other horses.

Judge and Scribe: In this type of competition, each horse and rider receives an individual time to execute their test of choice. The Judge gives you his or her complete attention and evaluates each movement. The scores are listed on each line and comments dictated for each segment of the test. An assistant called a "Scribe" sits next to the judge notating each comment and score. The judge should never have to take his focus off of you and your horse while you are riding your test.

Registration and Closing Date: Decide which classes are right for you and register before the **Closing Date**. Show Managers need time to schedule classes and this deadline is usually the week before the Show Date. Unlike rail classes, horse and rider teams go into the arena one at a time. Each test has a time limit in which you are expected to complete the required movements.

A few days after the Closing Date you will be given your **Ride Time**. Plan ahead and arrive early to warm your horse up and be mounted and ready to enter the arena when the horse and rider listed ahead of you goes in.

Tack: Open competitions offering Gaited Classes often allow English saddles of varying types but snaffle bits are a must for the Dressage Arena. Our standards of tack follow USDF Approved Guidelines and do check as they can change from year to year.

Clothing: Helmets should be worn for every discipline and this type of competition is no exception. Neatness is important and hair should be gathered and tucked under the helmet or in a hair net or "bun-warmer". Breeches and polo shirts are usually appropriate in open competition but do check with the show manager for details. Tall boots or half chaps stabilize the lower leg for more consistent leg aids as well as serve to complete your outfit.

As you become more involved in this discipline and showing in the Dressage Arena you may decide to complete your turnout with more formal dress boots and a Dressage coat. But most open shows do not require formal attire at Intro and Training Levels from those just starting to compete.

Grooming: Braiding the horse's mane is important for a few of reasons. First, it shows respect and consideration toward the judge by allowing a clear view of both sides of the horse's neck when evaluating the horse's movement and bend. Also, it keeps the mane from impeding your cues and getting tangled in the reins. And finally, it gives a tidy appearance and allows you and your horse look your best as a team.

Unlike the colorful ribbons used in our Gaited rail classes, trailing mane and forelock ribbons are not appropriate for Dressage Shows. As always, it is important to be neat and well turned out with all of your bridle straps and keepers neatly tucked in, your horse should be immaculately groomed and your boots and tack polished. Nothing should interfere with the Judge's eye nor pull her focus away from the movements of the horse and the equitation of the rider.

Get Still, Relax and Enjoy the day!

Relax and remember: You are what you are. The point of the Dressage Test is to give you a snapshot of you and your horse; what you have accomplished together and where you are that day. The Judge is there to affirm, measure and report her findings regarding what you are doing well and what needs improvement.

It is an exciting time for our Gaited horses and Dressage Competition. Open Dressage Show Series all over the country are including and inviting our gaited breeds to join them in this educational and challenging discipline.

The principals learned in this wonderful course of study are timeless and serve as the basis of communication and movement with our horses.

Top Ten Reasons to study Dressage:

1. Evaluates horse and rider communication

2. Builds connection between horse and rider.

3. Prepares horse and rider for infinite number of challenges in an infinite space on the trail

4. Encourages Rhythm and Impulsion and therefore better Gait and Cadence

5. Bends and Straightens the horse to improve suppleness, fitness and stamina

6. Provides a sequential program for setting mounted and academic goals.

7. You get a handful of written homework with every test!

8. Connects you the learner to the wisdom of both ancient and modern masters of the art of horsemanship.

9. You never run out of lessons, there's always something new to learn.

10. Creates an ever more capable and symmetrical horse and an ever more mindful and purposeful rider.

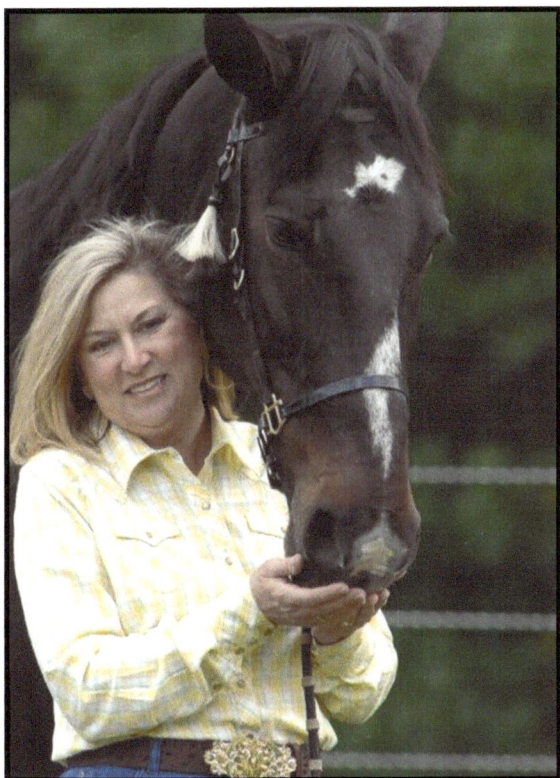

References & Recommended Reading

"Classical Training for the Paso Gaited Horse", Elizabeth Creamer and Gwyneth McPherson

"Gaitkeeper Mutation in DMRT3 Gene" Stichting International Foundation for Animal Genetics

"Horse Gaits, Balance and Movement", Susan Harris

""Lessons In Lightness", Mark Russell

"The Nature of Horses, Their Evolution, Intelligence and Behaviour", Stephen Budiansky

"On Horsemanship", Xenophon

"Ride The Right Horse", Yvonne Barteau

"Training the Gaited Horse from the Rail to the Trail", Gary Lane

"Walking Horses, Biomechanics, The Stepping Pace and the Spirit of Dressage", Lee Ziegler